Playing It Straight

*A Practical Discussion
of the Ethical Principles of the
American Society of Newspaper Editors*

JOHN L. HULTENG

Published by the
American Society of Newspaper Editors

Distributed by

Old Chester Road
Chester, Connecticut 06412

**Funded by the
Gannett Foundation**

Copyright © 1981 by John L. Hulteng
Library of Congress Card Catalogue Number: 81-65984
ISBN: 0-87106-955-5
Manufactured in the United States of America
All Rights Reserved

Contents

Foreword
Preface
Acknowledgments

THE PRINCIPLES

Preamble   3
Article I: Responsibility   5
Article II: Freedom of the Press   15
Article III: Independence   25
Article IV: Truth and Accuracy   35
Article V: Impartiality   43
Article VI: Fair Play   51
Conclusion   67

Recommended Reading   68

APPENDIX

Newspaper Ethics in Practice   71
   Samplings from Daily Papers   71
   The APME Code of Ethics   77
   UPI: A Policy Statement   80
   The Sigma Delta Chi Code of Ethics   82
   The ASNE Statement of Principles   85

ASNE's Board of Directors and Ethics Committee   87

Index   88

Foreword

The press faces no greater problem than that created by public doubt about its adherence to high principles and ideals. Some accusations of unethical conduct are groundless. Others, unfortunately, are not. No thoughtful observer questions the need to achieve greater fidelity to accuracy, fairness and balance. That is the objective of the American Society of Newspaper Editors in publishing this book.

Disagreement exists even among journalists over what constitutes ethical practice. Thus, dogmatic assertions would serve little purpose here. Instead, the author has charted those areas of clear danger and those of controversy in an attempt to stimulate thought and discussion and in this way to assist reporters, editors and publishers in avoiding unwitting transgressions.

Whatever success this book enjoys must be credited to its author, John L. Hulteng. He gave unstintingly of his rich wisdom and wide experience and worked through his vacation and recovery from an illness to meet the printer's deadline.

The task of seeing that this book receives the attention and study it merits is beyond the reach of ASNE's Ethics Committee. That effort is left to journalists and others who are interested in the profession's welfare and the quality of its contribution to society.

Claude Sitton, Chairman,
ASNE Ethics Committee

Preface

The purpose of this book is to suggest, through discussion of cases, some ways in which the Statement of Principles of the American Society of Newspaper Editors may be implemented in newspaper practice.

The approach has been selective, of necessity. Within the space limitations set, only a few aspects of journalistic ethics could be considered, and those but briefly. No attempt has been made to offer precise guidelines; each reporter, editor and newspaper faces different situations and no simple or absolute rules can apply to all.

In most of the cases cited in the text, the names of individuals and publications involved have been omitted; the purpose of the case citations is not to point the finger of blame but to illustrate some of the problems involved in applying principles in day-to-day practice.

J. L. H.
Palo Alto, California
January 1981

Acknowledgments

The Ethics Committee of ASNE is especially appreciative of the wise advice, able assistance and enthusiastic encouragement given this project by Thomas Winship, ASNE's president. It thanks ASNE's Board of Directors, the society's executive director, Gene Giancarlo, and its legal counsel, Richard M. Schmidt, Jr., for their help.

The committee expresses special appreciation to the Gannett Foundation, whose financial support made this book possible. The committee also is indebted to the generosity of the editorial cartoonists whose work illustrates the book, to Robert H. Phelps and Gerald D'Alfonso for long hours spent in editing it, to the guidance of Robert W. Chandler, William Hosokawa and Donald J. Sterling, Jr., and to Charles B. Everitt of The Globe Pequot Press, Inc., for courtesies and considerations.

C.S.

THE PRINCIPLES

Gene Basset, *Scripps-Howard Newspapers*

PREAMBLE

The First Amendment, protecting freedom of expression from abridgment by any law, guarantees to the people through their press a constitutional right, and thereby places on newspaper people a particular responsibility.

Thus journalism demands of its practitioners not only industry and knowledge but also the pursuit of a standard of integrity proportionate to the journalist's singular obligation.

To this end the American Society of Newspaper Editors sets forth this Statement of Principles as a standard encouraging the highest ethical and professional performance.

Don Wright, *The Miami News*

ARTICLE I
•
RESPONSIBILITY

The primary purpose of gathering and distributing news and opinion is to serve the general welfare by informing the people and enabling them to make judgments on the issues of the time. Newspapermen and women who abuse the power of their professional role for selfish motives or unworthy purposes are faithless to that public trust.

The American press was made free not just to inform or just to serve as a forum for debate but also to bring an independent scrutiny to bear on the forces of power in society, including the conduct of official power at all levels of government.

Although the Constitution doesn't provide for it in so many words, the American press has acquired through the years an indispensable role in the functioning of our democratic system. As former *Wall Street Journal* editor Vermont Royster put it, "That very phrase, 'Fourth Estate,' implies that we are part of the self-governing process of our society." The media provide the information that the electorate needs in order to make intelligent decisions at the ballot box and to keep tabs afterward on the stewardship of officeholders. Inherent in this function are vast power and concomitant responsibility. Neither should be abused.

The power and responsibility are shared by all persons involved in the processes of gathering and disseminating the news: reporters, photographers, editors and publishers. The decision-makers high in the editorial heirarchy obviously wield power over the shape of the news; but so do reporters, who are the first to sort out details and facets of a news event, discarding some and building others into the story.

It is an abuse of journalistic responsibility when a publisher exploits the news columns of his publication to further a favored candidacy or issue, or to attack an opponent. Some examples:

• The head of a chain of newspapers sent his editors a heavily editorialized attack on a president and requested them to give it prominent display as news. When two editors in the chain balked and wanted to give the material the more appropriate label of "editorial," they lost their jobs.

• The publisher of a small daily fired the editor and a reporter on his paper because they publicly disagreed with his decision to suppress campaign information concerning certain candidates he opposed.

• The publisher of a statewide daily acquired international notoriety for his practice of stacking the decks in the news columns of his paper in order to influence the politics of his region, assigning disproportionately large amounts of news space to candidates he favored and printing chiefly negative reports about those he opposed.

Less obvious and less widely noticed—but no less objectionable—are instances of abuse of the professional role and media power by reporters and editors.

• A business page editor reached an agreement to join the staff of a large regional corporation within two years. During the remainder of his time on the paper he took every opportunity to give strongly favored play to news about his future employer.

- A sportswriter irked by a player's refusal to give locker-room quotes began to ride the player in his copy, using the sports page to further a personal vendetta.
- An editorial writer deliberately faked letters to the editor in order to suggest public support for editorial positions taken by the page.
- A reporter eager to make a quick reputation at the paper hyped up quotes from a news source, hoping to generate controversy that would give her the chance to produce more interesting copy and thereby win attention and promotion.

The fact is that persons involved in the news business, at every stage along the processing pipeline, have daily opportunities to abuse the power of the press. It is easy enough to shade a news item or tilt a headline in order to indulge a bias or score a point. American readers are fortunate that most of the time most journalists resist those temptations.

Defanged Watchdogs

Some violations of press responsibility come through as omissions rather than commissions.

For example, the obligation to bring scrutiny to bear on the activities of government may be evaded in various ways.

On some newspapers—usually small ones—a "don't-rock-the-boat" philosophy has been enshrined. Sloppy practices in local government are overlooked, zoning grabs are not reported or deteriorating conditions in the schools are ignored because the publisher doesn't want controversy in the news columns. The publisher would rather not alienate local leaders or jeopardize advertising revenues. So the news report is deliberately focused on innocuous routine events involving lots of names and no rhubarbs. The balance sheet stays healthy but the basic mission of the press is unfulfilled.

The failure of mission can be laid to reporters as well:
• To the police beat reporter who gets on such chummy terms with his news sources that he winks at inefficiency or worse rather than blow the whistle.
• To the Washington correspondent who knows of a congressman's disabling drinking problem but keeps any hint of it out of stories so as not to risk losing access to a profitable capital pipeline.

Admittedly, in both of these cases the journalists involved are expected to identify and walk a narrow line. The police reporter and the Washington correspondent well know that part of their job is to cultivate sources as diligently as possible; their value to the paper depends on their ability to get an inside track on the news. Yet they must not be co-opted; they must not take on the colorations and the value systems of the persons or agencies they are assigned to cover. It takes a clear eye and a sure foot.

Hard Judgment Calls

Those reporters and editors whose job it is to scrutinize the activities of government on behalf of the public often face perplexing and momentous choices. Some information that is unarguably newsworthy may possibly jeopardize national security; in such circumstances, what is the journalist's obligation—to print the news or suppress it in the national interest?
• During wartime newspapers have willingly held back on information detailing troop or ship movements to avoid giving aid to the enemy. Yet, overall figures on deployment have been reported, as during the Vietnam conflict, on the ground that the public needed to know the extent of our involvement.
• Editors of *The New York Times* learned in advance of the plans for the Bay of Pigs invasion of Castro's Cuba in 1961, but after President Kennedy requested

The Times to kill the story, the newspaper deleted references to the coming invasion as a Central Intelligence Agency operation, removed information regarding its imminence and reduced the headline on the story, which led page one, from four columns to one. Later, *The Times,* its publisher and editors, and the President were not at all sure that the decision to downplay the story had been the correct one.

• After Iranian militants seized the U.S. embassy in Tehran in 1979 and took a group of American hostages, reporters for newspapers, networks and newsmagazines were aware for weeks that another group of six Americans had secretly taken refuge in the Canadian embassy. But no word got out until the Canadians had succeeded in spiriting the group to safety, and no one questioned the propriety of the news suppression.

• When the magazine *The Progressive* proposed to publish an article about the inner workings of the hydrogen bomb in 1979, government spokesmen tried to stop the story, contending that it would reveal military secrets and endanger national security. The reactions of editors around the country were mixed: some expressed concern about the security issue while others accepted *The Progressive's* position that the "secrets" involved had already been published and that in any event the American people needed to be better informed about the country's weapons policy. On one point virtually all the editors agreed: the government's use of a court order to prevent publication of the article represented an unacceptable resort to prior restraint.

Presumably no journalist would willfully endanger lives or jeopardize the nation in order to break a story. But government officials are quick to invoke national security as an argument, often without sound justification and sometimes more to cover up an embarrassing blunder than to safeguard a legitimate secret.

That argument can force reporters and editors into making harrowing judgment calls they might prefer not to face.

What Tactics Are Fair?

Judgment calls can sometimes involve questions of means and ends. To some journalists, newsgathering methods that might be considered unjustifiable in normal situations may seem necessary when the stakes are high.

For example, it is a reasonable assumption that most journalists would not steal or commit other crimes to get news stories. Yet in the celebrated case involving the Pentagon Papers in 1971, several of the nation's most distinguished editors found themselves dealing, without formal authorization, with copies of secret government documents. Years earlier some of the same editors had denounced the dissemination to the press by Sen. Joseph R. McCarthy, the unscrupulous anti-Communist zealot, of information derived from confidential files. But the Pentagon Papers detailed the way in which the nation had become entangled in the bloody nightmare of Vietnam; the public had an overriding right to know the story as detailed in government records, however those records came to light. Or so most editors reasoned.

Crusades for certain causes can serve the public interest if the reporting is thorough and balanced and the articles are clearly labeled. Even so, ethical questions related to tactics of newsgathering sometimes arise when reporters take on other roles in order to get at an elusive story. In 1977 reporters for the *Chicago Sun-Times* set themselves up in business as the proprietors of The Mirage, a neighborhood bar, in order to see what they could find out about graft in the city's inspection system. The reporters filmed and taped civic officials accepting bribe money as the price for ignoring sanitary and construction violations at the bar. Some editors felt that the deception involved entrapment. Others defended it as commendable journalistic enterprise, contending that this was the only way the story could have been obtained.

In other cases reporters have represented themselves as police officers or doctors in order to get news sources to open up. After an accident at the Three Mile Island nuclear plant in 1979, a reporter obtained a job at the facility to get some firsthand information about security practices there.

Editors who debate these and like cases seem to be able to agree that there is not much wrong in reporters taking on additional roles in order to get at the news so long as no deliberate deception is involved. A reporter who passes himself off as a policeman would be behaving unethically; a reporter who applies for a job at a mental hospital or a nuclear facility to check on conditions at the institution would not be open to criticism so long as she does not claim for herself medical or technical qualifications she does not actually possess.

The dividing line thus drawn is admittedly indistinct, and some editors argue that the only sound policy is to stay aboveboard at all times; any role that involves concealment of the reporter's professional identity would compromise the integrity of the reporter and the publication.

Not-So-Innocent Interlocks

The ASNE Statement of Principles calls on journalists to bring scrutiny to bear not only on government but on all the "forces of power in society." In discharging that obligation, newspapers have investigated the role of corporations in polluting air and water, the activities of manufacturers whose products posed hazards to consumers, the tactics of labor leaders who failed to respect the rights of union members and the methods of special-interest groups whose goals promoted racism and bigotry.

But the vigilance of the press with respect to forces of power in society can sometimes be suspect. If a newspaper group were owned by an oil company, for example, readers might understandably wonder how searchingly the reporters would scrutinize the activities of the oil company. When the directors who make policy for the newspaper group also sit on the boards of banks, insurance companies, auto manufacturers, schools, conservation societies, symphony orchestras and lobbying groups, might these interlocking relationships be reflected in the top-level decisions that determine how the newspapers in the group function?

It can be argued that such entanglements of top management are far from the day-to-day operations of the newspaper. But that distance may not be a sufficient insulation. The knowledge that the newspaper group is owned by an oil company could represent a pervasive influence on reporters and editors dealing with a story about the oil industry, even though no director may have handed down a go-slow warning from on high. And to some staff members, the publisher or editor who is a trustee of a university, a pal of the mayor or a member of a committee to help a special-interest group appears to be sending a signal for the special handling of articles on such subjects. Even if the staff members maintain a scrupulously impartial approach to such coverage, readers who know of the interlocking relationship may doubt the reality of that impartiality. Where the responsibility of the press to keep an eye on the power forces in society is involved, the appearance of impropriety may be as damaging as an actual ethical lapse.

The watchdog function is neglected, too, when a reporter or editor railroads a press release into the paper with no more than a touch of cosmetic editing.

Public relations material can contain legitimate news, and that news belongs in the paper. But any handout, whether from a corporation, a school district or a labor union, almost always has some self-serving aspect. An uncomfortable development is tidily buried in verbal excelsior, a product plug is deftly inserted or a policy position carefully clouded over so that its true implications won't be apparent. The legitimate news in PR handouts should be channeled into the paper, just as news obtained from other sources. But the special pleading aspects of the material must be weeded out. Too often, they slip by. When they do, the responsibility of the press to scrutinize the forces of power in society has not been met.

Steve Benson, *The Arizona Republic*

ARTICLE II

•

FREEDOM OF THE PRESS

Freedom of the press belongs to the people. It must be defended against encroachment or assault from any quarter, public or private.

Journalists must be constantly alert to see that the public's business is conducted in public. They must be vigilant against all who would exploit the press for selfish purposes.

Most journalists are aware that they have an obligation to defend freedom of the press when it is under attack; the obligation comes with the job.

But meeting that obligation can occasionally involve painful consequences and difficult decisions for a publication or for an individual.

There are, of course, some threats to press freedom that are obvious and for which standard responses have been worked out.

When a city council chairman tries to close a meeting to a reporter, the reporter knows that she is expected to stand her ground as long as possible and then leave only under protest. She will try to get the news of the meeting from participants, if that is feasible, and she will report the incident to the city editor, who will initiate the appropriate legal steps. If there is an open-meeting law in the jurisdiction, that may decide the issue. If there isn't, the paper can very likely stir up public opinion through news coverage and editorial comment to persuade the city council to mend its ways.

When Mayor Jane Byrne of Chicago tried to intimidate a *Chicago Tribune* reporter by ordering him to vacate his desk in the city hall newsroom, he simply stayed put. His paper and his colleagues in the news media gave the ouster attempt (in June 1980) plenty of coverage. The mayor technically had the power to have him ejected physically, since the newsroom space was city property. She didn't do that. She backed down. Similar power plays aimed at muzzling a reporter or cutting off access to news have been tried by numerous civic officials, but they all came a cropper when their tactics were thoroughly aired in the press.

One of the most potent weapons the press possesses in combating attacks on its freedom is full exposure of the threat—with the confidence that the public, once it knows the situation, will not tolerate it.

But there are some practical limitations on the effectiveness of this response by the press.

What worked for the Chicago reporter, with a powerful paper behind him and media friends supporting the cause, may not work in a small-town setting. Whether in small town or big city, the tactic of appealing to public opinion to frustrate a threat to press freedom will be successful only as long as the public continues to recognize the indispensability of the press as watchdog.

That recognition is neither universal nor enduring. Many leaders of the press worry that it has been eroding in recent years. When then-Vice President Spiro Agnew unleashed his biting, alliterative attacks on the press in the late 1960s, he triggered alarming support from many sectors of the public. The situation improved for the press during the Watergate era, when its watchdog contributions were dramatically highlighted. But a good many thoughtful persons feel that resentment and suspicion of the press remain. Public acceptance of the historic role of the press may not be so solid and predictable as assumed.

To prevent further erosion, editors and reporters should refrain from excessive or unjustified appeals to public opinion. A knee-jerk invocation of press freedom every time some public official or special-interest representative criticizes the performance of the press will only harm the cause. The press is just as subject to legitimate criticism as any other agency in society. Cry "Wolf!" only when a genuine predator is on the prowl.

Facing the Subpoena

Threats to press freedom take many forms and come from many quarters. Often they are far more complex and more difficult to counter than the closed-meeting try by the city council or the pettish gesture by the mayor.

In recent years, law enforcement agencies have increasingly attempted to co-opt the press as a source of criminal evidence. Reporters or photographers may gather facts that a district attorney lacks. If the material is published, there is no problem. Anyone can make use of it. But some background information collected by reporters may not be suitable for publication. It cannot be fully checked out, or it may have libelous implications. In the pursuit of such unpublished material authorities have obtained subpoenas demanding reporters' notes or photographers' negatives.

In the 1960s there were only about a dozen or so instances involving subpoenas for reporters' notes. In 1970-71 there were 150 such cases, but by 1976 the annual tally had risen to 500.

(In 1978 the Supreme Court ruled, in a case involving the Stanford University student newspaper, *The Stanford Daily,* that law enforcement authorities could resort to a search warrant to rummage through a newsroom for evidence.

(However, in 1980 Congress passed and President Carter signed remedial legislation which, within the year, would protect the work product of journalists, including their notes, film, tapes, etc., from surprise searches by federal, state and local law enforcement agencies unless the journalist were a suspect in a crime. But the power of subpoena remains, a process that provides for a hearing on the essentiality of the news material as evidence.)

Any citizen has an obligation to provide testimony if such testimony is necessary to the administration of justice. But the journalist has the additional obligation to defend freedom of the press, and that freedom is certainly jeopardized when the press is commandeered to serve as an adjunct of the law enforcement system. Reconciling the two obligations is often difficult and sometimes impossible.

• In some cases, newspapers have mounted step-by-step legal resistance to subpoenas calling for the submission of reporters' notes or the negatives of unpublished photographs. There have been some victories, some compromises and quite a few defeats. All confrontations, whatever the outcome, have imposed substantial, even crippling, legal costs on the newspapers involved.

• Some journalists have chosen to accept contempt judgments and jail sentences rather than yield to court orders requiring the production of notes or negatives.

• Some editors have reacted by stripping their newsrooms of note and negative files that might attract a subpoena.

There is no formula to guide journalists who are

confronted with court or police demands for material to be used in evidence. The ends of justice, of course, deserve consideration (e.g., when a defendant is on trial for his life and a reporter has the only access to evidence that could free or hang him). But in most cases authorities very likely can develop the desired information by their own investigation. Their efforts to use the press as an adjunct to the law enforcement apparatus ought to be resisted. The publishers who shouldered massive legal expenses and the reporters who temporarily gave up their personal liberty to that cause made the responses they felt were appropriate to the circumstances. Similar responses no doubt will be made in the future, as individual publications and individual journalists try to carry out what they perceive to be their professional obligation.

The Public's Business

If the defense of press freedom has become increasingly difficult for journalists, so has the effort to ensure that the public's business be conducted in public, particularly business involving the courts.

A 1979 U.S. Supreme Court decision *(Gannett, Inc. v. DePasquale)* held that the public, and thus the press, had no right of access to a criminal pre-trial hearing under the Sixth Amendment. During the months that followed, numerous lower-court judges issued rulings reflecting that decision. Most involved pre-trial hearings, but some resulted in the closing of actual trials and the withholding of announcements of verdicts.

A second Supreme Court decision a year later *(Richmond Newspapers, Inc. v. Virginia)* cleared the air somewhat, in that it affirmed, under the First Amendment, the public's right to attend trials; it did not, however, modify the earlier finding with respect to pre-trial hearings.

The two decisions represented the latest phase of a long-standing controversy arising out of seemingly contradictory thrusts of the First and Sixth Amendments to the Constitution. The First prohibits government interference with individual liberties and the functioning of the press; the Sixth provides that every accused person shall have the right to a public trial by an impartial jury.

Bench and bar argue that pre-trial coverage, and some forms of coverage while the trial is under way, may bias prospective or already selected jurors and thus destroy the defendant's Sixth Amendment right. First Amendment supporters respond that failure to keep the news spotlight steadily focused on the workings of the justice system may lead to abuses of the rights of individuals and a denial of the right of the public to be informed properly about the public's business. They also point to the Sixth Amendment which states that the accused "shall enjoy the right to a speedy and public trial."

Until the *Richmond* decision, the Sixth Amendment provided the only explicit constitutional reference to a public trial. The *Gannett* case held that, at least as to pre-trial proceedings, only the accused had that constitutional right, and not the people or the press. But with *Richmond,* the court held that the public's right of access to criminal trials is found implicitly under the First Amendment.

However, the fair trial-free press debate goes on. Advocates of the Sixth Amendment deplore sensationalized press coverage that might damage the rights of defendants. Supporters of the First Amendment insist that liberty and justice suffer when law enforcement or judicial agents, regardless of their motives, operate in secrecy.

Attempts to resolve the enduring controversy have taken various forms. Bar-press committees have formulated codes for guidance, and some newspapers subscribed to them as far back as the early 1960s. In addition, judges have resorted to the various remedies available to them when they believe that the press may invade the Sixth Amendment guarantee (e.g., change of venue, delay of trial, sequestering of the jury, etc.).

Some of these attempts have been at least partially successful. The bar-press committees, in particular, offer a forum in which the inherent conflict between the two constitutional provisions can be examined calmly and the rights and wrongs of all parties can be sorted out. But the basic issue remains, as the two Supreme Court decisions emphasize. The press has a responsibility to oppose, with all resources available, the trend to closed or non-public judicial proceedings, including the focusing of public attention on the various evils that can develop in a system of closed justice.

Frustrating the Users

Article II of the ASNE Statement of Principles urges journalists to be vigilant "against all who would exploit the press for selfish purposes." That is a large order; would-be exploiters are both numerous and ingenious. Some examples:

• Politicians organize media events, occasions of dubious or nonexistent news value, in the hope that the press will cover them and thus provide the pols with cost-free exposure.

• Demonstrators, both foreign and domestic, time and tailor their activities to press availability, hoping to direct disproportionate public attention to their causes. Campus crowds obligingly wave placards, shout slogans or smash windows when photographers are ready to record the action. During the 444-day crisis over the seizure of American hostages in Iran which began in November 1979, mobs outside the

United States embassy whipped up a frenzy on cue when the press appeared on the scene, then disbanded when the reporters left.

• Manufacturers of food products feed a steady supply of inviting recipes to food section editors, all featuring the companies' products either specifically or generically. The manufacturers hope to build demand for their soup seasoning or canned tuna without having to pay for advertising space.

In these and in many similar attempts to exploit the press, journalists have to pick their way with care. They want to prevent the newspaper from being used, but they don't want to overlook genuine news elements that may be present.

The politician's press conference may indeed be contrived, but it should be covered on the off chance that something worth reporting might come up. If nothing does, the reporter ought to be professional enough to scratch the story, not file some empty copy to justify having spent time on the event.

Some demonstrations may be calculated fakery, but others may represent the only way a voiceless group can present its causes. The former deserve short shrift, the latter often belong in the news report.

Many recipes featured on food pages do serve a useful purpose. But mention of brand names ought to be pruned away and quantity references keyed to specific packaging sizes of individual products ought to be converted in order to minimize the exploitation.

Although someone who comes asking for newspaper coverage may have some authentic news to offer, it is a pretty safe bet that the person is also trying to use the press to some degree for a vested interest. It is the reporter's job to get the genuine news into the paper and to winnow out the self-serving aspects.

Exploitation of the press is not confined to outsiders. Reporters who try to *create* news by writing speeches for public figures, by inciting demonstrators to step up the tempo of violence, by agreeing to ask questions planted by a source or by promising a candidate coverage if he or she will make an outrageous attack on an opponent have grossly misused their role.

"This could get us into trouble . . . That's too controversial . . . No, we couldn't say this . . . We'd offend readers with that . . . Oh, my gawd . . . We'd lose advertisers with this."

Paul Szep, *The Boston Globe*

ARTICLE III
•
INDEPENDENCE

Journalists must avoid impropriety and the appearance of impropriety as well as any conflict of interest or the appearance of conflict. They should neither accept anything nor pursue any activity that might compromise or seem to compromise their integrity.

Men and women in the news business cannot allow their motives to become suspect. Their sole purpose should be to serve the basic ethic of journalism: to inform the public as honestly and as fully as possible about events in the community and the world. They must not use their role to serve some other purpose or interest.

Well and good. But as a practical matter, just what constitutes impropriety for a journalist? How do you recognize when a damaging conflict of interest is arising?

If a news source you see every day—say the county treasurer—offers to buy you a cup of coffee, is your integrity as a reporter compromised if you accept? Suppose it's an offer to buy a drink instead of a cup of coffee? Or a bottle of 12-year-old Scotch? Or the use of a mountain cabin for the weekend? At what point, if at all, have you become so beholden to your generous news source that you can no longer be counted on to cover the office even-handedly?

If the publisher is appointed to a state commission set up to assign names for rivers and mountains, will the impartiality of the paper come under question? Suppose the publisher takes a seat on the board of regents of the state university? On the board of directors of a local machine tool manufacturer? Or is elected to public office? In what circumstance, if any, has the publisher compromised his or her professional integrity and that of the newspaper?

The simplest approach to such problems is, of course, the absolute one. A Chicago police officer, talking about patrolmen who succumbed to bribery, observed: "It all begins with a cigar." Once the moral boundary is crossed, the size or nature of the bribe is immaterial. That point of view is reflected in many newspaper codes that sternly prohibit a journalist from accepting *anything* of value from a news source.

But an absolutist policy can lead to awkward and unrealistic situations. A war correspondent, for example, can hardly cover a battlefront action without resorting to military transportation. And, on a more mundane plane, should you reject the cup of coffee proffered by the county treasurer, or insist on paying for your lunch when you cover the weekly Rotary meeting? The city editor expects you to maintain friendly relations on your beat; a holier-than-thou stance won't make that easy.

Built-in Hazards

Yet anything *other* than an absolutist approach may be difficult to live with, privately or professionally. For by its nature journalistic work involves numerous situations with the potential for "impropriety or the appearance of impropriety." Some examples:

• Sportswriters who also serve as paid official scorers for baseball games can find themselves in complex conflict-of-interest situations almost any night in the box. And reporters who accept travel, food and lodging from the teams they are covering have brought their impartiality under suspicion.

• Travel writers who accept junkets to Hawaii or Brazil financed by an airline or a resort may forfeit their readers' confidence in the objectivity of their reporting.

• Food writers run similar risks. At a national chicken cooking contest sponsored by two food-product manufacturers, 40 of the 60 editors attending accepted food, transportation, drink and hotel rooms from the sponsors. (Their bosses aren't always careful, either. The annual Washington conventions of the American Society of Newspaper Editors used to feature elaborate cocktail parties sponsored by auto manufacturers. These have been discontinued. But there are still lunches and other occasions for newspersons underwritten by groups with some special-interest ax to grind.)

• The editor or editorial writer who accepts the invitation of the State of Israel to tour the Middle East at Israeli expense may come back with an improved understanding of that crisis-ridden region but also with a built-in bias—or at least the appearance thereof.

• Each year some 300 contests sponsored by various trade, commercial or special-interest agencies are open to journalists. There are prizes for the best writing about cigars, furniture, oil and numerous other products, services or causes. The prizes represent the equivalent of a quarter million dollars in cash each year. How many news stories are shaded and shaped so that they can double as winning entries in such contests?

It is not the case, to be sure, that every freebie or prize is offered with the specific purpose of corrupting journalistic morals. Photographers who covered the

1980 Winter Olympics all received packets of goodies from a camera manufacturer, presumably to encourage them to use its products. The cocktail parties underwritten by paper companies at publishers' conventions represent a pitch for newsprint sales, not news space. And the annual trade association contests are usually presented as efforts to recognize specialized journalistic excellence after the fact, not as subtle advance influences on the news report.

But whenever journalists—including photographers and publishers—accept something of value from any outside source, the action may well give rise to the assumption that something or someone is being bought. Such assumptions are too costly to risk.

So in any situation that seems borderline, the journalist must be able to provide honest negative answers to two questions:

Would acceptance of this proffered favor (consideration, gift, junket, freebie) cause me to give special handling to news about the giver?

And, even if this first answer is no, would knowledge of the exchange give my readers the *impression* that I have somehow sold out? You must pass both parts of the litmus test to stay out of trouble.

Getting Involved

Not all conflict-of-interest problems stem from freebies, nor do they all involve sports, food or travel writers. General assignment reporters, editors, publishers and owners have their problems, too.

Most such problems arise when journalists become linked in some way with persons, agencies or causes that they and their newspapers are covering as news.

The linkage can be casual or formalized. It can be motivated by commendable civic spiritedness or individual greed. But the end result is a duality of allegiance that in many cases threatens journalistic integrity.

The ethical rights and wrongs in this area are particularly difficult to sort out. Journalists cannot be expected to live antiseptic lives, cut off from all forms of involvement except their professional one. They belong to political parties and churches; they join social groups; their children attend schools, some of them public, some private, and perform in school plays or on sports teams; their wives belong to bridge clubs, their husbands to golf clubs, and they may even play in tournaments. It is possible to plot a scenario in which such conventional and homely involvements with the community might pose a conflict of interest for a journalist, but the risk is not great.

However, you do not have to go much beyond that level before running into perplexing questions.

Suppose, in addition to belonging to a political party, a reporter actively supports a particular candidate to the extent of making a contribution, putting a bumper sticker on his car and driving the candidate to a neighborhood rally. One reporter lost his job for doing just that.

Or suppose that a reporter assigned to cover a candidate becomes romantically involved with the candidate, yet continues to report news about campaign activities.

Or suppose that a reporter helps out a candidate or an officeholder by writing press releases and giving media advice. That practice was once commonplace in American journalism but now is considered unacceptable on most newspapers.

At the far end of the unacceptability scale, it would seem, would be political officeholding by journalists while still working at their craft. They, their colleagues and their publications would be hopelessly compromised.

Yet, a kind of double standard sometimes seems to be in effect. In small towns, particularly, the editor or a reporter may indeed hold office on the city council, the county commission or the school board. And on both large papers and small ones, the publisher may regard himself or herself as an exception to the rule that keeps other staff members out of politics.

Such journalist-officeholders may not themselves be directly involved in covering news growing out of those offices. But the fact of their participation in political affairs will unquestionably affect coverage by their fellow staff members who do have those beats. The conflict of interest is classic. So why is it permitted to arise?

Journalists who do take an active role in politics, even to the extent of holding office, defend their involvement on two grounds. The hands-on participation, they argue, will provide them with an insight and understanding that will in the long run better equip them to cover or comment on politics. And they also contend that they have an obligation, as well-informed citizens of the community, to shoulder civic responsibilities: Who else in town is better qualified?

But most journalists are unwilling to buy such arguments. When it comes to reporters, editors *or* publishers dabbling in party politics or seeking political office, the risks to integrity and reputation are too great to run. In fact, as A.M. Rosenthal of *The New York Times* once put it, "A journalist pretty much has to give up any kind of political activity beyond voting. That's the price we pay for being newspaper people."

Even *Good* Causes

The price may be almost as high when the journalist's involvement is not with politics but with civic agencies or causes, some of which may seem patently blameless and non-controversial. Some illustrative instances:

• A reporter who was elected president of a neighborhood improvement association was asked by his editors to resign the post because it might require him to take a position on a complex zoning issue his paper was covering.

• A Midwest publisher was criticized by his own managing editor in an ombudsman column because the publisher had been leading a campaign to get the state legislature to build a publicly financed sports stadium adjacent to the newspaper's building.

• An editor of the *Los Angeles Times* declined an invitation to become a member of a local council promoting peaceful solutions to school integration problems because he felt that the paper's coverage of the issue would lose credibility if he became identified with the council.

• In Florida, several prominent publishers contributed heavily to a campaign to oppose the establishment of casino gambling in the state. Staff members of the papers involved protested, feeling that their impartiality in covering news about the campaign had been brought into question.

In these and in many, many similar cases the pivotal issue is conflict of interest. And, as with the journalist's involvement in politics, there are varying points of view.

Some editors and reporters feel that the concept of the "sanitized" journalist, totally removed from all entanglements with civic agencies and causes, is unrealistic. As Eugene Patterson of the *St. Petersburg Times* observed: "We damn well have civic responsibilities, and we'd be poor citizens if we didn't act on them."

At the other pole are those who feel that persons who cover the news cannot afford in any way to be identified with causes, individuals or organizations that are news-makers. There's no such thing, they argue, as being just a little bit pregnant. One editor has even cut himself off from purely social contact with former classmates who have become prominent in civic, business or political affairs to avoid any possibility of compromise.

In search of solid footing on a middle way, some journalists reason that distance is the answer; a sportswriter, say, or a business editor could serve on a United Way board without damaging the paper's credibility, while a reporter covering the agency could not.

Others feel that journalists' involvement is defensible if the readers are fully informed about it in advance; the editors and staff members of *The Lewiston Tribune,* an Idaho daily, once listed in detail and in print all the business, civic and political affiliations of everyone on the paper's news side.

But perhaps the most practical approach is for the individual journalist to ask the question: "Just why am I being invited to join this agency's board (or committee, or association, or fund drive)? Because I am so able and qualified? Or because someone, somehow hopes to exploit the fact that I work for the paper—to get favorable coverage, to apply leverage on a third party or to provide useful window-dressing?" An honest answer ought to furnish as much guidance as any right-minded journalist needs.

Similarly pointed questions also ought to be asked of themselves by:

—publishers who own substantial stockholdings in businesses or industries covered by their publication's reporters;

—editors invited on Defense Department tours of military installations;

—and Washington correspondents who are taken up socially by Capitol Hill or Cabinet bigwigs.

The conflict-of-interest problem comes in all sizes and guises. Everyone in the news business has to contend with it sooner or later.

Bob Englehart, *The Hartford Courant*

ARTICLE IV
•
TRUTH AND ACCURACY

Good faith with the reader is the foundation of good journalism. Every effort must be made to assure that the news content is accurate, free from bias and in context, and that all sides are presented fairly. Editorials, analytical articles and commentary should be held to the same standards of accuracy with respect to fact as news reports.

Significant errors of fact, as well as errors of omission, should be corrected promptly and prominently.

In any business as fast-paced as newspapering, errors are inevitable. Reporters try to avoid them, editors try to weed them out and proofreaders try to catch them, but the misspelled name, the transposed age and the garbled quote somehow slip through the nets. They are usually unintentional, simply the result of craft conditions. But they can be costly, both to those persons who have been misrepresented in the public prints and to the paper itself.

For every time a reader spots an error the paper becomes, for that reader and sundry friends and relations, a less credible messenger. "If they can't even spell my name right, how many other mistakes have they got every day?" That sort of erosion of reader confidence is cumulative and costly. Mistakes can be expensive in tangible terms, too, when they give rise to libel actions that high-priced lawyers must try to defeat.

So there are the soundest of reasons behind the old International News Service injunction to "Get It First, But First Get It Right." The extra few moments needed to double-check represent a sound professional investment.

There are, however, some lapses from journalistic accuracy that cannot properly be labeled honest errors. And they can be particularly destructive of an institution's reputation.

• An editor in a small town once published a vivid account of an illegal cockfight in a rural neighborhood—only to be forced to admit later that the whole story was a fake. It had been lifted, in its entirety, from another publication in another region. The editor's lame explanation that an episode very like the one reported had probably occurred recently somewhere in the region did not mend the damage. Reporters who deliberately jazz up quotes to heighten their impact are dealing in the same brand of disreputable fakery.

• A metropolitan daily once printed a column headed "Our Mayor Speaks" and presented it as though it were the unvarnished personal observations of the then mayor, a frequent target of press criticism. It was actually the work of a regular columnist on the paper and was intended as a parody. But the spoof was not fairly labeled, and many readers took it for real.

• Two stringers for a regional daily filed a story, with picture, of a farmer who had produced a star-spangled, red-white-and-blue pickle. A wire service picked up and distributed the story, which, of course, was cut out of whole cloth; the two stringers described it as a "tongue-in-cheek" article. Both lost their jobs with the newspaper.

Begging Pardon

Whenever an error does get into print, whether the result of a typo or a hoax, there ought to be a prompt correction. And it must be an honest correction, properly labeled, candidly worded and prominently featured, not swept under the rug next to the classified section.

• A newspaper in a college community ran a story under a four-column, 48-point head charging that the university president was cutting student services "to Beef Up Coaching Funds." That wasn't the case at all, and the paper ran a correction the next day—but the correction was a tiny two-paragraph item in a back section under an 18-point head. The story acknowledged that what the president had really said was that he intended to beef up teaching funds at the sacrifice of administrative services.

• In another instance, a paper ran a long feature on a local youth who had completed college on an accelerated schedule. At a key point in the story the student was quoted as saying, "It's easy if you have a golden mind." A target of ridicule, the boy complained to the paper, which in due time printed a very small item noting that what he had really said was: "It's easy if you have a *goal in mind*."

In both cases the newspapers involved had complied technically with the obligation to correct an error. But in neither instance was it a wholehearted correction that significantly mended the damage. As a practical matter, most corrections cannot be run in exactly the same place and under the same-size headline display as was the case with the original error. But there are ways to make the correction effective, and most newspapers in recent years have begun to use them.

Regular correction spots, for example, are used by about three-fourths of large-circulation papers and a majority of smaller ones as well. A standing head, clearly labeled "Correction" or something similar and in a fixed position each day (say, on the second page or at the end of the news summary), calls attention to errors that are being corrected. This gives fair emphasis to the corrections without having to deck them out with the same-size headline and placement as the original story.

Still, the record isn't always good. A survey early in the 1970s asked editors how many corrections were run in their papers in an average month. Two-thirds of them responded "one to five." It seems a pretty safe assumption that even the most meticulous paper prints more than five consequential errors in a month's time (the carefully edited *Wall Street Journal* publishes between 30 and 50 "corrections and amplifications" monthly). At the time of the editors' survey, many errors simply were not being corrected. In more recent years the batting average has been higher.

Some errors are caused by omission rather than commission, and there has been a certain reluctance by some editors to acknowledge that omission of critical material—even unintentionally—should be pointed out to readers.

Most journalists understandably hate to admit that they have made mistakes. They rationalize that many errors are trifling and that the complainers are nitpicking. But to the individual reader who has been wronged, the misstep is major and the need for a correction imperative. And an honest admission may do much to mend a credibility gap that the publication can ill afford.

"You're Not Playing Fair!"

Error correction can be a clear-cut matter; a misstatement of fact can be quickly identified and, to at least some degree, rectified. But dealing with bias that has seeped into the news report tends to be far more complicated.

TRUTH AND ACCURACY

For one thing, determining when and if the news is biased is an exercise in subjectivity. The journalist, attempting to act on behalf of the whole readership of the paper, selects out of a news situation those elements that would seem to be of interest and consequence to the greatest number of readers. But each individual reader views the news through a personal frame of reference, perceiving bias if the account does not conform with and reinforce personal values and priorities. Many reader complaints about bias stem from such perceptions, assuming tilting of the news report when there has been none.

In other instances, however, the complaints may be more justified. It once was routine practice for newspapers to give more news space and bigger headlines to those candidates favored by the papers' publishers and editorial pages. Such blatant deck-stacking is uncommon today, although it does occur now and then. More often, bias shows up in other ways. Some cases:

• Senator Henry Jackson of Washington, running for the Democratic presidential nomination, addressed a rally of about 50 persons in a small Florida community. A wire service photographer got a shot of the scene from within the audience. The photograph showed only three persons in the foreground, one a small boy on a bike, and just beyond them the senator on a podium, earnestly declaiming. When the photograph was published around the country without fully explanatory cutlines, it made the candidate a figure of ridicule, a hapless campaigner who drew crowds of three. Other photographs of the rally had been taken which showed most of those attending, but the editors' choice of the shot depicting only the trio was widely cited as reflective of press bias against Jackson.

• When schools opened one fall in Boston at a time when desegregation had just begun, the reaction to the start of busing took several forms. Almost all the children cooperated without incident. There were some scattered episodes of violence by non-students; there were also instances of peaceful acceptance by affected parents. Some of the photographs available showed rock-throwers; others showed groups kneeling in prayer. Although a pairing of pictures to draw the contrast would have been possible, many papers chose instead to feature only the rock-throwing episodes. The linkage between school busing and violence had become a stereotype, and, again, the editors' choices served to reinforce that stereotype and give readers a distorted impression of the news reality.

• The incumbent candidate in a political campaign was invariably the beneficiary of the journalistic convention that incoherence and sloppy grammar will be smoothed over in a quote before it appears in the paper. But his challenger was given no such brushup treatment; his every blooper and crudity came out in print just as he had committed them. Readers who had heard both men on the stump and knew them to be equally fallible had justification for believing that the paper was slanting the news to favor one side.

If "good faith with the reader is the foundation of good journalism," as Article IV asserts, reporters and editors must learn to be sensitive to the potentialities for bias in every part of the news hole. A headline, a picture, a descriptive phrase in a story—any one of them may be enough to light the "tilt" sign and give readers reason to believe that the news has been deliberately tainted.

Dwane Powell, *The News and Observer*

ARTICLE V
•
IMPARTIALITY

To be impartial does not require the press to be unquestioning or to refrain from editorial expression. Sound practice, however, demands a clear distinction for the reader between news reports and opinion. Articles that contain opinion or personal interpretation should be clearly identified.

Generations of journalists have wrangled among themselves over the reality and the sanctity of the distinction between news and opinion. The wrangling intensified in the 1950s and 1960s with the advent of interpretive reporting and the several versions of "new journalism."

The debate has not been a simple, two-sided one. The arguments have been less over absolutes than over various shades of gray. Most of those involved were able to agree that the "old" journalism, with its insistence on complete objectivity and rigid compartmentalization of factual news and expression of opinion, needed modification. There has been less unanimity about how much modification was needed and what directions it should take.

As long ago as the 1940s a national Commission on Freedom of the Press warned that "It is no longer enough to report *the fact* truthfully. It is now necessary to report *the truth about the fact*." More recently, James Reston of *The New York Times* observed that

"You cannot merely report the literal truth. You have to explain it."

Those are pretty awesome injunctions. How, as a practical matter, do you go about identifying "the truth about the fact?" Philosophers have wrestled unsuccessfully with that one for centuries. And in explaining the meaning of the literal truth (assuming that you *can* first identify it), how far can you stray from the old journalistic distinctions without disservice to the reader?

Perhaps, as many in the news business contend, the ideal of total objectivity is indeed unrealistic. Reporters and editors cannot be expected to take a completely disinterested approach to the news; it just is not humanly possible. But does that mean that the *concept* of objectivity is outmoded? Because an ideal is just beyond your grasp, do you stop trying to reach toward it?

It is unarguable that the news has become very complex and the reader clearly needs help in understanding it. The journalist can offer much help, in the form of interpretation and backgrounding. But does that require that news and opinion be blended into a hybrid of new journalism and served up with a warning of *caveat emptor*? Is not the reader still entitled to truth in packaging?

Gatekeeper or Advocate?

For the journalist trying to fashion responsible answers to these bothersome questions, there may be some help in a study undertaken by a University of Chicago sociologist, Morris Janowitz. He discovered that most journalists today tend to follow one of two models of professionalism: the gatekeeper and the advocate.

Those who see themselves as gatekeepers consider it to be their job to "detect, emphasize and disseminate that which was important." The gatekeepers still respect the concept of objectivity, though they concede that they cannot be purists, and they try to maintain a distinction between news and opinion.

Those who embrace the advocate model believe that they have an obligation to act for those elements of society that do not have spokesmen and have little access to the channels of power. The advocate journalists' ideal is that "of the lawyer and almost that of the politician" and for them "the search for objective reality yields to a struggle to participate in the socio-political process by supplying knowledge and information." (Morris Janowitz, "Professional Models in Journalism: The Gatekeeper and the Advocate," *Journalism Quarterly,* 52 No. 4 [Winter 1975])

In the Janowitz model the gatekeepers would seem to be faithful to the basic journalistic ethic of informing the public as honestly and as fully as possible of events in the community and the world. The advocates appear to be serving another purpose as well, that of helping to shape events in order to improve society.

Some newspaper people, of course, have always worked at that second purpose, as editorial writers and columnists. Now reporters and other news-side staff members are claiming a piece of the action, too. What are the implications for the journalistic institution, and for readers?

A Risky Option

Letting opinion infiltrate the news columns on a wholesale basis is a high-risk exercise for newspapers. During the 20th century, journalism's strongest claim to a special standing in society has rested on its reputation for providing as accurate and undistorted a news report as possible. Newspapers have also provided opinion, entertainment and advertising. But they have been labeled as such, and they have been—and remain—secondary in importance to the news function.

If newspapers were to abandon the goal of an unbiased news report and become organs of advocacy and opinion like *National Review* and *The New Republic,* they might well forfeit an important part of their function. They would not be as readily recognized as impartial proxy for the public in scrutinizing the sources of power in society. Reader confidence would be eroded and would likely splinter into the sort of fragmented support characteristic of the 19th-century partisan press.

Readers would be left to piece together an approximate picture of reality by ranging across the spectrum of opinion journals and striking an average from their various versions of "news."

That would not, of course, be a new situation. It would be very much like the brand of journalism available in many countries around the world. But it would be a sharp and lamentable retreat from the concept of responsible and undistorted journalism that has been developed in this country through the generations.

Blurring the Line

So there remain sound reasons for the language of Article V, for the maintenance of a "clear distinction for the reader between news reports and opinion." And journalists, both old and new, need to be wary of practices that blur that distinction. Some examples:

• Certain journalists, in an effort to make their copy more vivid and meaningful, resort to the devices of the fiction writer. They "reconstruct" a conversation between figures in the news even though they have no solid evidence to go on. The exchange seems plausible; it *could* perhaps have taken place, but in fact there is no way to be sure whether it did or did not. Or they invent a composite figure to exemplify a type. Such a composite figure is presented as a real-life person, but actually consists of bits and pieces of the mannerisms or experiences of various real persons, blended into a composite that in the journalist's judgment is representative and can serve as a protagonist or vehicle in a news story. It is a partly true depiction and a partly fictional one. These devices have no place in the news columns; they deceive and cheat the reader.

• Other new journalists take what they describe as an alternative approach. They operate on the assumption that conventional journalism has long reported the news from the viewpoint of the dominant forces in society; it has been the official spokesman who has been quoted, the Establishment frame of reference that has been reflected. So the alternative writers and reporters deliberately concentrate on aspects of the news that they feel have not been adequately covered in the past. They seek not a balanced report, but one *unbalanced* in a way intended to make up for past omissions—a kind of affirmative action in the news columns, with economic and political rather than sex or race implications. In the process, they are inevitably distorting the flow of current news.

• Both old and new journalists indulge in a practice that falls in a gray zone between interpretation and flat-out lying: excessive reliance on anonymous sources.

News accounts from Washington or the state capital are often studded with "sources close to the State Department . . ." or "a Presidential aide said . . ." or "supporters of the governor acknowledged privately . . ." and similarly faceless and nameless spokesmen; a flesh-and-blood source may never show up in the story. It is sometimes necessary and helpful to make use of information supplied on condition that there be no direct attribution. But it is very easy to succumb to the temptation to cheat with such material. Anonymous quotes can be doctored to make them more biting or dramatic, or they can be made up from first to last to fit a given news situation and support the premise of a story. As with the composite character, they have an appearance of reality. Someone *might* have uttered them; in the context they seem to belong. But how is the reader to know whether there really is a "source close to" or a "White House aide" behind the quotation? Could the reporter be padding the story with made-up comments to give it more heft?

It is far better to go with genuine quotations from named sources who are in a position to complain if they have been misrepresented. Then the readers have some guarantee that they are getting honest reporting. The appearance of impropriety can be as damaging to the paper's integrity in the case of faceless sources as it is in instances of conflict of interest.

Jeff MacNelly, *The Richmond News Leader*

ARTICLE VI
•
FAIR PLAY

Journalists should respect the rights of people involved in the news, observe the common standards of decency and stand accountable to the public for the fairness and accuracy of their news reports.

Persons publicly accused should be given the earliest opportunity to respond.

Pledges of confidentiality to news sources must be honored at all costs, and therefore should not be given lightly. Unless there is clear and pressing need to maintain confidences, sources of information should be identified.

Often in reporting the news, journalists must decide whether to publish information that will cause embarrassment or pain to persons involved directly or indirectly. Sometimes the public's need to know about the event will be so obvious that the sensitivities of individuals affected must be disregarded. In other, less clear-cut circumstances, the journalist must weigh values, as a judge does in a courtroom, to determine whether newsworthiness should take priority over the individual's right to privacy. And the journalist, facing a deadline, must go through the weighing process with far less time for deliberation than the judge on the bench.

Some in the news business try to sidestep the responsibility. They cite editor Charles Dana's philosophy in the 19th century that whatever the good Lord permitted to happen Dana was willing to print in his paper. But passing the buck to the Lord is too simplistic. Responsibility for making difficult judgments does indeed rest with reporters and editors.

News or Exploitation?

Meeting that responsibility gives rise to more and trickier ethical calls than almost any other aspect of newspapering. A look at some cases will suggest the range and complexity of these calls:

• A girl from a small West Coast town died in an accidental fire on a university campus in another state, where she was a student. The story that came over the wire service reported that her body had been found at 5:30 a.m. in a burning fraternity house. Should the hometown paper report the circumstances of the death, or simply say that the fire took place in "a campus residence" and spare the grieving family some additional pain? The editor decided to print the full story, reasoning that it would inevitably become known in the community anyway and that blurring the account would serve little purpose and might constitute a breach of journalistic responsibility.

• An even more difficult decision faced another editor. The daughter of a family in the community had been murdered in Washington, D.C., and the episode had been reported in the hometown newspaper. Then along came a more detailed account that had been published in a Washington daily; this story revealed that the girl had been working as a prostitute at the time she was killed. Should the second story also run in the hometown paper? It did, and the editor was barraged with the criticism of outraged readers complaining about morbid sensationalism. But most editors who commented supported his decision, contending that how she came to be killed was a necessary part of the story, even though it would inflict shock and pain on the community in general and on the girl's family and friends in particular.

• Whether the cause of death should be routinely included in obituary stories is a question that comes up almost daily for reporters and editors, not just in dramatic murder cases. If the story is of a death by accident or violence, the cause will of course be an integral part of the account. But most deaths are caused by illness, and in many instances the families would prefer that the nature of the final illness not be noted in the story. However, readers have a strong interest in knowing the cause of death; they want to be aware what ailments are striking down their fellows ("There, but for the grace of God, go I"). Despite this reader-interest factor, many journalists respect family wishes as a matter of common courtesy and omit the cause of death, unless there are compelling reasons for disregarding the request (e.g., an epidemic or other threat to public health, or a coroner's verdict fixing the cause of death).

• A 14-year-old girl was dying of cancer. Her dearest wish had been to visit a coastal resort community far from her Midwest home. Such a visit was made possible by a gift from a benefactor, and the girl and her mother came to the resort town. The situation was loaded with pathos and human interest; by any standard, it clearly deserved a story. But it got far more than that.

For nearly two weeks the resort-town newspaper followed the girl day by day, in photographs and copy. She was shown at the airport, being greeted on arrival. She was shown visiting the beach, riding a horse, posing with dancers at a night club. As her condition worsened she was photographed at the hospital, where she sat up in bed to greet her stepfather, flown out for a last reunion. Her benefactor also arrived and there were more hospital photographs, revealing the baldness caused by the radiation treatment for her cancer. Daily headlines chronicled the pathetic saga as the suspense built.

The final accounts described her departure from the resort-town airport in semiconscious condition and her death in an ambulance on the way to her home.

It was a tear-jerker of a story from beginning to end. It was also a classic instance of press exploitation of personal tragedy, an ethical lapse not only on the part of the resort-community editors but also by many other papers around the country that picked up and carried the stories and photographs as they came over the wire.

Many situations arise involving media exploitation of children or other relatives of famous persons. When the son or daughter of an actor or a mayor has a minor tangle with the law, the story has obvious reader interest even though it might not rate even a line if there were no celebrity connection. But what about invasion of privacy? What about the injustice of exploiting the relationship for the sake of news?

• A reporter for a metropolitan daily learned that the son of a United States senator was in financial straits and was getting food stamps. There was nothing illegal about the situation, but the fact that a senator's son was reduced to this necessity seemed newsworthy. So the newspaper gave the story heavy play. The senator protested, pointing out that his son was an adult, living his own life, and that what he did or didn't do had nothing to do with the father's public career. Later the paper's ombudsman acknowledged in a column published in the paper that running the story had been wrong. Wrote the ombudsman: "In my memo to . . . editors on the matter I said I saw the story as 'the urge to expose gone wild.' "

• The daughter of a senator was arrested on a minor drug charge and thereby earned headlines. But she was 41 at the time, not a child still part of the senator's household. And even if she had been 14 rather than 41, should her arrest have been a news item?

On the other hand, if a senator's relative is involved in an activity that compromises the senator's effectiveness as a public servant, there can be little question about the need to publish. And politicians who parade their families on the campaign trail as a part of their appeal to the voters greatly weaken any later claim to privacy for the activities of those same family members.

Where to Stop?

By its nature, investigative journalism, much in vogue in this post-Watergate era, impinges on the lives of individuals in the news. Almost all of the information turned up by the press in pursuit of wrongdoing and corruption is certain to cause pain and anguish to someone when it gets into print. In most cases the material nevertheless must be published, in the public interest. But when the hunt is up, reporters and editors sometimes have difficulty judging how far to go and where to stop.

• The editors of a metropolitan daily were given information that a union official then leading a crippling strike in the community's largest industrial plant had at one time been a member of the Communist Party. The editors were urged to publish the information, since it might discredit the union leader and break the strike. A reporter assigned to investigate discovered that the information was accurate, but that the union leader's tie to the Communist Party had been short-lived and had been broken off many years ago. The editors decided that the early affiliation was not a legitimate part of the current news situation and, therefore, did not publish the story. The decision was taken despite the fact that the president of the struck corporation was also a member of the board of directors of the newspaper.

• Reporters working on a story about a virulent anti-Semitic group in their city uncovered the fact that a leader of the organization had been born of Jewish parents and had been raised in that faith. His beliefs had changed over the years and he had eventually joined the racist group, concealing his background from the members as he had worked his way to the leadership post. When the reporters informed him that they had found out about his origins and intended to publish the information, he pleaded that the story not be used. It would, he said, destroy the career he had built for himself; he threatened to commit suicide if the story were published. The reporters consulted with their editors and it was decided that the story should run. When it did appear, the man killed himself. In the aftermath, the writers and editors involved stood by the decision to publish, pointing out that the story was newsworthy and that it had to be published in the public interest. Other editors around the country generally supported the decision, although some said that they might have felt an obligation to warn the man's doctor before going ahead with the story.

Editors of another paper recall two instances when they consulted with doctors about suicide threats from persons who were to figure in news stories; in both cases the editors decided not to run the stories in question because the doctors had indicated that suicide was a distinct possibility.

• A reporter was preparing a background feature on a 71-year-old businessman who had just made a $500,000 gift to a local university. In the course of his investigation the reporter discovered that the donor had served prison time as a youth after being convicted of forgery and grand larceny. In the years since his release from prison he had led a successful and blameless life as a business executive and family head. Should the early misstep be mentioned in the story? Was it a legitimate and necessary part of the current news situation? The prison background not only came out in the story, it was the burden of the headline. The paper's editors were sharply criticized, not only by persons in the community but by their fellow editors elsewhere in the country. In the judgment of the critics, this was a situation in which the sensibilities of the individuals involved should have outweighed considerations of newsworthiness.

Identifying Tags

Such a basic reportorial task as the selection of labels and tags to identify persons in a news story can affect readers' sensitivities.

In an earlier era when such titles as Mr., Miss and Mrs. were commonly used in newspaper copy, it was the practice on some Southern papers to omit these honorifics when black persons were mentioned in news stories; such blatant discrimination is now discredited. Not many years ago reporters routinely sprinkled their copy with such references as "willowy blonde" or "curvaceous stewardess"; now nearly all news writers manage to avoid such offensive excesses, although some milder sexist references persist.

Racial identification tags are used by most newspapers only when they are necessary to make the story meaningful. When a criminal is being sought by the police, the description obviously should be complete ("A 20-year-old white male, wearing . . ."). But when a golfer wins a tournament or a student is awarded a scholarship, race normally would not be considered a necessary part of the identification.

Editors who experimented with a policy of always using racial identification in any story which reported a creditable achievement by a minority-group member typically discovered that this was not welcomed by minority readers, as the editors had assumed it would be; it was viewed instead as a patronizing gesture.

In trying to avoid unnecessary racial labeling, reporters occasionally lean too far, omitting identification tags that serve a useful purpose. In one such instance, a North Carolina jury acquitted two Nazis and four Ku Klux Klan members charged with killing five Communist Workers Party supporters. One newspaper's account of the verdict, compiled from wire service reports, did not mention the race of either the defendants or the victims. It did describe the jury as "all-white" and that partial clue, combined with the Southern setting and the involvement of KKK members, left many readers with the impression that the shooting victims had been black and the defendants white. In fact, four of the slain were white and one black. Using too few racial identification tags may in some cases inflame rather than reduce tensions.

It isn't with racial labels only that journalists encounter touchy identification problems.

A war veteran who had saved President Ford's life during an assassination attempt in San Francisco in 1975 was identified in a newspaper column as a homosexual. The story was picked up across the country. The veteran was dismayed by the revelation; although his sexual orientation was known to his associates in the city's gay community, his relatives elsewhere in the country had not been aware of it until the story broke. He complained that this was an unwarranted invasion of his privacy.

The newspaper writer who used the homosexual angle felt it was necessary to the story because it offered a possible explanation for the failure of the White House to extend formal thanks to the veteran. Additionally, some spokesmen for the gay community in the city were eager to have the man's homosexuality become known generally, since it would enhance the image of gays to have an acknowledged hero in their ranks. But did these factors outweigh the individual's sensitivity about the revelation?

Questions such as these did not often confront earlier generations of journalists. But in today's social climate they do arise, and with increasing frequency. In attempting to deal with them, reporters and editors try to apply the yardstick of relevancy: if the sexual orientation of a figure in the news is a fact that is essential to an understanding of the story, it should be reported. Thus, if a murder victim is shot because he attempted to seduce another man, his homosexuality is properly part of the story; if the same man is shot by a burglar he encounters in his home, the victim's sexual orientation has no news significance.

But not all distinctions are that clear-cut. Sometimes the relevancy yardstick can be difficult to read.

A homosexual ran for a municipal office in San Francisco. He made no secret of his orientation; on the contrary, he was bidding for the support of the city's many gay voters. Reporters had no problem covering the campaign.

But suppose that a homosexual candidate is running in a Midwestern city, and suppose that he considers his sexual preference a personal matter and seeks to avoid disclosure. Should he nonetheless be identified as a gay in news accounts of his candidacy? Does the voting public have an overriding right to know? Would it make a difference whether he were running for the city council or for governor? Or for President?

There are no easy answers to these questions, either in consensus or rule of thumb. The only responsible approach is a conscientious weighing of values and circumstances, case by difficult case.

Photo Problems

The need to weigh values arises often for photographers and picture editors. Should the highly newsworthy accident photo be used, even though it shows a mangled body? Should the dramatic shot of a woman's horrified reaction to the sight of her murdered husband be published—or filed unused because it trades on an individual's suffering? Should the series of pictures showing the torture and execution of Ethiopian rebels be printed as graphic evidence of the savagery of the desert war, or rejected as too hideous for a general-circulation audience? Decisions about which shots to use and which to pass can be taxing. Some instances:

• An East Coast paper published two photos of a car-bicycle accident. One showed a middle-distance view of the scene moments after the accident. The body of a small boy lay on the pavement, near the crumpled bike. The boy's mother knelt beside him and an ambulance attendant could be seen in the background. It was a powerful composition and it effectively conveyed the tragedy of the episode. The second published photograph was a multi-column close-up of the mother lifting her dead son's head in her arms; her features were twisted with pain, her mouth open in a cry of anguish. Use of the first photograph, although it would unquestionably cause distress to the child's family, could be justified on grounds of newsworthiness. However, what about the closeup shot? It certainly had impact and readers no doubt paused to look at it. But was it essential to the story? Or was it an indefensible exploitation of a moment of personal agony?

• The Associated Press Managing Editors Assn. once presented a panel of its members with two photographs of a fire scene. One depicted the gutted shell of the burned home with its vacant windows and blackened walls. The other showed a father clutching his head in a spasm of grief; his children had burned to death in the home. Which picture, the editors were asked, would you use to illustrate the fire story?

The shot of the grieving father was chosen by 86 percent of the editors. Many of them acknowledged that the picture represented an invasion of privacy but that its use was nonetheless justified because it emphasized the human dimension of the fire, not just the property damage shown in the blackened building shot.

• Consider a case that is partly true and partly hypothetical. Three teenagers were waterskiing at a country lake in the Northwest. Their boat overtook a canoe just as the skier was sweeping across the wake, and the taut ski rope decapitated one of the canoeists. Such an episode did happen. There were no photographers present, but suppose there had been and that they had obtained an assortment of shots from which an editor later had to choose. One photograph very likely would have been of the headless body slumped in the canoe; others would have depicted the general scene but not shown the body, and one surely would have been a mug shot of the teenager who had been at the controls of the ski boat, shock showing in his face. If you were the editor, which pictures would you have run?

The one of the body in the canoe would undoubtedly have had the greatest news value, but it would also have been deeply offensive to the family and friends of the victim and just too gruesome for most readers. The mug shot would have tended to point the finger of blame at the teenager; would that have been fair to him at a time when the accident was yet to be investigated? The overview pictures, while less powerful than the others, would probably have been the ones most editors would have elected to publish.

• A photographer covering a fire shot a remarkable

sequence of pictures of a baby-sitter and her charge falling from a collapsing balcony as they tried to escape the blaze. In the last frame the spread-eagled form of the baby-sitter was shown just before she hit the ground and was killed. The photographs, which won a Pulitzer Prize, were widely used and everywhere aroused a storm of reader criticism: ". . . repulsive . . . outrageous . . . atrocious . . . worst possible taste." Yet very few of the editors had misgivings about using the compelling photographs. They were obviously newsworthy, the editors reasoned, and they also served as a warning to the public about the need to improve fire safety precautions. Several years later a similarly dramatic sequence of pictures of a high-wire artist falling to his death was widely used by editors.

• When Mount St. Helens erupted in Washington state, one of the photographs taken the next day from a helicopter showed a pickup truck. In the truck's bed lay the body of a boy, his legs jutted upward and his arms folded across his body. For two days editors of a major newspaper in the area debated as to whether to use the photograph. Did this grisly scene convey as nothing else could the nature of the St. Helens disaster? Was it fair to the family and friends of the dead boy, and the families of the many other dead, to thus freeze in their memories this terrible moment? Was the picture a legitimate part of the news coverage or sensationalist exploitation? The decision, when it came, was by no means unanimous, but it was to publish. Again there was an outburst of reader indignation: ". . . barbaric . . . unimaginable . . . subhuman." But most editors around the country who had the chance to use the picture did run it, endorsing by their action the original decision. (To be sure, editors in other regions had no readers in the eruption zone and thus had fewer factors to weigh.)

• Shortly after an abortive attempt to rescue the American hostages held in Iran, pictures were made by an Iranian photographer of the scene on the desert where eight American servicemen had died when two of the rescue planes collided accidentally. The Associated Press desk in New York received four of the photographs for possible distribution to member newspapers around the country. Three of them showed the wreckage and two bodies lying face down. These were distributed and given widespread play. A fourth shot was held back by the editors at AP. It was a close-up of a charred body in the debris of the aircraft. Facial features, though burned, were identifiable; the blackened arms reached up pleadingly. The AP editors judged that in the case of the fourth picture newsworthiness had to give way to considerations of taste and decency. There was no dissent from editors who later saw the photograph. (Would the AP decision have gone the other way had the body been that of an Iranian, not an American?)

Problems also arise when photographs are cropped for size or better composition—or when they are combined with other photographs in a composite display. Such surgery should never result in a distortion of the reality captured by the original photograph(s). In addition, such practices as posing pictures in a newspaper office and misrepresenting them as having been taken in a prison or a medical facility (as has happened) are equally indefensible.

Decisions about photographs and their use will always be difficult and controversial for journalists. The rights of individuals and the sensibilities of the readers must in every case be weighed against news values, and a balance struck that is at once professional and humane.

"I Didn't Say *That!*"

Balances must be struck, too, in dealing with quotations. Ideally, reporters place direct quotation marks only around the exact words uttered by a speaker or news source. But unless the reporter always uses a reliable tape recorder and has an unlimited news hole to work with, the ideal may be hard to attain.

As a practical matter, there are usually some compromises. Prolix comments are boiled down; sloppy grammar and opaque phrases are cleaned up and clarified; key observations are plucked out to be used in the story, without the full, original context.

There are obvious hazards in all of these compromises. Both the news source and the reader may be badly served unless the reporter operates with a surgeon's precision and with the fairest of motives.

Most reporters and editors regard it as their responsibility to transmit without distortion the sense of what a speaker or news source said. If the comments cannot be cited in entirety, with complete and literal accuracy, their burden must be conveyed honestly. It is never justifiable for a journalist to make up quotations, however plausible or characteristic, or to edit a source's comments so that their thrust or meaning is altered in any way. And any paraphrase or summary without direct quotation must be scrupulously faithful to the meaning of the full original utterance.

(Admittedly, even with the reporter's best efforts to play fair, the source is almost certain to complain about misquotation or misrepresentation. Seeing in cold print what you have tossed off casually during an interview, or in the heat of an exchange, can be a jolting experience for any of us; the typical reaction is: "I didn't say *that*!" Some sources could not be convinced even by a tape recording playback.)

Shielding Sources

Article VI of the ASNE Principles calls on journalists to respect pledges of confidentiality made to news sources, and to extend such pledges only when there is "clear and pressing need." This puts an awkward but inescapable burden on reporters and editors.

Most of the time, news writers routinely identify the sources of information or opinion included in the story. Without such identification the story is incomplete and the reader has no basis for judging whether the information should be considered trustworthy. There are, however, circumstances in which it becomes necessary for a reporter to promise a news source confidentiality in order to gain access to information that would otherwise be unavailable. Bureaucrats who want to blow the whistle on grafting superiors or uncover another Watergate cannot afford to be named as the source of the charge for fear of retaliation; if they can be sure they will not be fingered, they will provide the leads and tips the reporter must have to break the story.

But such pledges of confidentiality must be entered into only when there is no other way, for they put both the reporter and the paper at risk. Moreover, every attempt should be made to win agreement from confidential sources before publication that if the courts should order the journalist to name the source, the source will step forward and testify.

Some states have passed shield laws designed to support journalists in their claim of source confidentiality. Shield laws, however, will not deflect a court order after a judge has decided that the public interest requires disclosure. In addition, attempts to invoke the First Amendment in confidential source cases have been rejected by the Supreme Court.

So journalists and their papers are left with grim choices. Is the story important enough to justify extending a confidentiality pledge? Can the pledge be maintained, even if, as has happened, a jail sentence for the reporter and a cumulative fine for the paper are in prospect?

Delaying actions may be fought, public opinion rallied and compromises bargained for, but in the end both personal liberty and institutional solvency may be on the line. If the stakes are high enough, the risks must be taken. But they should never be taken lightly.

"I HAD NO IDEA THE ASSOCIATION FELT THIS STRONGLY ABOUT ETHICS CODE VIOLATIONS!"

Pat Oliphant, *The Washington Star*

CONCLUSION

The ASNE Statement of Principles concludes with the following:

These principles are intended to preserve, protect and strengthen the bond of trust and respect between American journalists and the American people, a bond that is essential to sustain the grant of freedom entrusted to both by the nation's founders.

If it is true that a free press is indispensable to the public because it provides a catalyst for the functioning of a representative system of government, it is equally true that the respect and confidence of the public are essential to the continued survival of a free press. The interdependence is organic.

Vermont Royster of *The Wall Street Journal* once wrote: "It cannot be said too often: Freedom of the press is not an immutable right handed down by God on Mt. Sinai. This precious freedom is only a civil right granted by the people in a political document. And what the people give they can, if they ever choose, take away."

The ASNE principles set out in general terms the standards the press must pursue if public confidence and trust are to be maintained. The several sections of this book have described a few of the ways in which these principles are given practical application. This discussion has been intended to be illustrative, but it is by no means comprehensive or all-inclusive.

Recommended Reading

The following books deal with journalism ethics from a variety of viewpoints, both professional and academic.

Casebier, Allen, and Janet Jinks Casebier, *Social Responsibilities of the Mass Media,* University Press of America, 1978.

Gerald, J. Edward, *The Social Responsibility of the Press,* The University of Minnesota Press, 1963.

Hohenberg, John, *A Crisis for the American Press,* Columbia University Press, 1978.

Hulteng, John L., *The Messenger's Motives: Ethical Problems of the News Media,* Prentice-Hall, Inc., 1976.

────── *The News Media: What Makes Them Tick?* Prentice-Hall, Inc., 1979.

Krieghbaum, Hillier, *Pressures on the Press,* Thomas Y. Crowell Company, 1972.

Merrill, John C., and Ralph Barney, editors, *Ethics and the Press,* Hastings House, 1975.

Rivers, William L., Wilbur Schramm and Clifford G. Christians, *Responsibility in Mass Communication,* 3rd edition, Harper & Row, 1980.

Rubin, Bernard, editor, *Questioning Media Ethics,* Praeger, 1978.

Swain, Bruce, *Reporters' Ethics,* Iowa State University Press, 1978.

APPENDIX

Newspaper Ethics in Practice

SAMPLINGS FROM DAILY PAPERS

Many of the nation's newspapers, large and small, have codes of ethics, some written, some understood.

Here are excerpts from some published codes. They are not intended to form a model code, for the infinite aspects of newspaper ethics and the nuances of the language do not permit the definitive statement. However, they are intended to demonstrate how the profession is attempting to govern itself while doing its job.

The newspapers represented here were part of a group solicited at random by the ASNE Ethics Committee.

Integrity

Editorial staff members of *The Tribune* are expected to avoid any compromises of their journalistic integrity. This must include even the appearance of compromise. The only special interest *The Tribune* will serve is the public right to know.

Common sense is the best guideline. . . . The code applies to management and staff alike.
—*Chicago Tribune*

Our newspapers strive for impartial treatment of issues and dispassionate handling of controversial subjects. They provide forums for exchange of comment and criticism, especially when such comment is opposed to our editorial positions. Editorials and other expressions of the writer's opinion and judgment are clearly labeled or identified as such for the reader.

Reporters sometimes write personal columns as well as news analyses including analytical and background material, but they refrain from expressing opinions about persons and issues they are covering in news stories.

Our newspapers report the news without regard for our own interest. We do not give favored news treatment to advertisers or special-interest groups. We report matters regarding ourselves and our personnel and families with the same standards we would apply to other institutions or individuals.

We identify ourselves and our organization to those from whom we are gathering information for publication. We do not plagiarize.

—*The Columbus (Ga.) Ledger and
The Columbus Enquirer*

We have an obligation to protect the public from all those who would mislead and corrupt and those in the news media must avoid the types of conflicts of interest which we would not tolerate elsewhere.

To this end we must always be willing to acknowledge errors of fact or implication and to correct those errors promptly and prominently. It does not honor us to plead ignorance nor to blame our news sources. The accuracy and honesty of what appears in our newspaper is our responsibility.

—*The Muskegon (Mich.) Chronicle*

Special Privileges

Press Credentials—Press cards and other similar credentials are issued solely to facilitate coverage of the news. They must not be used for personal purposes (e.g., to solicit favors or avoid enforcement of a law).

No member of Advertising, Circulation or any other department of the *News* shall claim press credentials or otherwise represent himself or herself as a reporter or editor.

—*New York Daily News*

Politics, Causes and Organizations

Work for a politician or a political organization, either paid or voluntary, is forbidden. Also forbidden is (1) holding public office or (2) accepting political appointment to any position *unless specific approval is given by the editor and publisher or the executive editor.*

There is no quicker source of misunderstanding and suspicion than the area of politics. We must not give any person reason to suspect that our handling of a story, editorial or picture is related in any way to political activity by a member of the staff.

—*The Courier-Journal and The Louisville Times*

Business Conflicts

1. Staffers should be sensitive to financial investments in companies they cover.

2. Staffers are not to use inside knowledge for their own personal gain.

3. Staffers are not permitted to enter into a business relationship with a news source.

—*Camden (N.J.) Courier-Post*

Use of Journal *Connections*—Employees must not use their position on the paper to their advantage in commercial transactions or for other personal gain. This specifically prohibits such practices as the use of *Journal* stationery for private business matters, letters of protest or similar dealings.

Investments—Financial investments or other outside business activities by *Journal* staff members that could conflict with *The Journal's* ability to report the news, or that would create the impression of such a conflict, must be avoided.

—*The Milwaukee Journal*

Taste

The Washington Post as a newspaper respects taste and decency, understanding that society's concepts of taste and decency are constantly changing. A word offensive to the last generation can be part of the next generation's common vocabulary. But we shall avoid prurience. We shall avoid profanities and obscenities unless their use is so essential to a story of significance that its meaning is lost without them. In no case shall obscenities be used without the approval of the executive editor or the managing editor or his deputy.

—*The Washington Post*

Gifts and Tickets

Freebies are freebies. There's no such thing as something for nothing. As professional journalists, we have no reason to expect, to seek, to want or to accept extra money, extra privileges, gifts, comps, favors or freebies from anyone.

We will no longer accept any complimentary tickets, dinners, junkets, gifts or favors of any kind. This includes movie passes, Orange Show tickets, tickets to circuses, books and records, new products, promotional gifts and toys, tickets to concerts, sporting events or any kind of show, lodging, press parties and meals of any kind.

—*The San Bernardino (Calif.) Sun*

We pay our own way. If it is newsworthy, we can afford it. If it is not, we can get along without it.

APPENDIX

Free tickets or passes to sports events, movies, theatrical productions, circuses, ice shows and other events for which the public is required to pay an entrance fee shall not be accepted by staff members or members of their households. Staff members who need to attend events for professional purposes shall pay for tickets and obtain reimbursement from *The Inquirer*. Staff members who are not required to attend movies or stageplays for review purposes shall not accept free access to them. Either in a theater or screening room.

—*The Philadelphia Inquirer*

Meals

The [ethics] committee recognizes that questions will arise about the acceptance of such things as a cup of coffee, a hot dog or a meal in an individual's home. The key to such situations is judgment. We don't want an individual employee or the company embarrassed by having a scuffle with someone over who will pay for coffee, or put in the position of embarrassing a hostess by demanding to pay for a meal served in a home.

In the case of the meal in the home we feel the code's statement "appropriate payment is sent later" means the customary thank-you note sent later.

We think it is logical that when one is invited by an individual or firm to lunch or dinner, it would be neither discourteous nor unprofessional to say something to the effect, "Yes, I'd be happy to meet you, but I want to say beforehand that our policy here on such things is that I pay for my own meal."

—*The Des Moines Register and Tribune*

Travel

No employee should accept a free trip, a reduced

rate or subsidized travel. The only exception is when traveling to an event at a reduced rate is the only means available.

An example would be an airplane chartered by a candidate for a statewide campaign swing for him and any accompanying reporters. *The Democrat* will pay its fair share of the travel costs. Staff members must consult with the executive editor or managing editor before accepting such arrangements.

Staff members may travel on chartered planes and take advantage of hotel arrangements or other services offered by a news source, provided *The Democrat* pays its share of the cost.

—*Tallahassee (Fla.) Democrat*

Sample Products

Samples of any products, including but not limited to books, records and tapes, generally should be regarded as gifts, in that those not used for news purposes should be donated to charity, with a letter to the giver explaining the action. Those samples, books, records, tapes, etc., that are desired for news purposes will be purchased from the sender by *The Star* at the standard retail price and will remain the property of *The Star*. Logistics will be handled by the editor's office. This policy includes all samples, including those sent to individual staff members at home or at work. (Samples should never be sold for personal profit.)

—*The Minneapolis Star*

*

The New York Times states its principle on the wall of its lobby:

> "TO GIVE THE NEWS IMPARTIALLY,
> WITHOUT FEAR OR FAVOR,
> REGARDLESS OF ANY PARTY,
> SECT OR INTEREST INVOLVED."

ASSOCIATED PRESS MANAGING EDITORS CODE OF ETHICS
For Newspapers and Their Staffs

This code is a model against which newspaper men and women can measure their performance. It is meant to apply to news and editorial staff members and others who are involved in, or who influence, news coverage and editorial policy. It has been formulated in the belief that newspapers and the people who produce them should adhere to the highest standards of ethical and professional conduct.

RESPONSIBILITY

A good newspaper is fair, accurate, honest, responsible, independent and decent. Truth is its guiding principle.

It avoids practices that would conflict with the ability to report and present news in a fair and unbiased manner.

The newspaper should serve as a constructive critic of all segments of society. It should vigorously expose wrongdoing or misuse of power, public or private. Editorially, it should advocate needed reform or innovations in the public interest.

News sources should be disclosed unless there is clear reason not to do so. When it is necessary to protect the confidentiality of a source, the reason should be explained.

The newspaper should background, with the facts, public statements that it knows to be inaccurate or misleading. It should uphold the right of free speech and freedom of the press and should respect the individual's right of privacy.

The public's right to know about matters of importance is paramount, and the newspaper should fight vigorously for public access to news of government through open meetings and open records.

ACCURACY

The newspaper should guard against inaccuracies,

carelessness, bias or distortion through either emphasis or omission.

It should admit all substantive errors and correct them promptly and prominently.

INTEGRITY

The newspaper should strive for impartial treatment of issues and dispassionate handling of controversial subjects. It should provide a forum for the exchange of comment and criticism, especially when such comment is opposed to its editorial positions. Editorials and other expressions of opinion by reporters and editors should be clearly labeled.

The newspaper should report the news without regard for its own interests. It should not give favored news treatment to advertisers or special-interest groups. It should report matters regarding itself or its personnel with the same vigor and candor as it would other institutions or individuals.

Concern for community, business or personal interests should not cause a newspaper to distort or misrepresent the facts.

CONFLICTS OF INTEREST

The newspaper and its staff should be free of obligations to news sources and special interests. Even the appearance of obligation or conflict of interest should be avoided.

Newspapers should accept nothing of value from news sources or others outside the profession. Gifts and free or reduced-rate travel, entertainment, products and lodging should not be accepted. Expenses in connection with news reporting should be paid by the newspaper. Special favors and special treatment for members of the press should be avoided.

Involvement in such things as politics, community affairs, demonstrations and social causes that could cause a conflict of interest, or the appearance of such conflict, should be avoided.

Outside employment by news sources is an obvious conflict of interest, and employment by potential news sources also should be avoided.

Financial investments by staff members or other outside business interests that could conflict with the newspaper's ability to report the news or that would create the impression of such conflict should be avoided.

Stories should not be written or edited primarily for the purpose of winning awards and prizes. Blatantly commercial journalism contests, or others that reflect unfavorably on the newspaper or the profession, should be avoided.

*

No code of ethics can prejudge every situation. Common sense and good judgment are required in applying ethical principles to newspaper realities. Individual newspapers are encouraged to augment these APME guidelines with locally produced codes that apply more specifically to their own situations.

A model code for members adopted by the APME Board of Directors, April 15, 1975.

UNITED PRESS INTERNATIONAL
A POLICY STATEMENT

United Press International's philosophy and purpose are outlined here by H.L. Stevenson, editor-in-chief, based on policy statements issued by the news service through the years.

United Press International is "dedicated to fair and balanced reporting of the news of the world in order to keep the people informed." These words are in the preamble of the charters of the UPI Newspaper and Broadcast Advisory Boards.

"The very reputation of the UPI will be riding on every word that leaves your typewriter," a manual for new employees states. "When you place the UPI logotype on a dispatch, you will be issuing both a personal and corporate guarantee to a UPI subscriber that it is accurate in every detail. That guarantee must not be given lightly."

The manual continues: "Do not confuse speed with excellence. The motto is, 'Get It First, But First Get It Right.' Make no mistake, the second half of that motto is the more important.

"Correct all errors swiftly and fully, showing what is being corrected and why."

Other areas of policy:

PRIVACY: Every person has a right to privacy. There are inevitable conflicts between this right and the public good or the right to know about the conduct of public affairs. Each case should be judged in the light of common sense, decency and humanity. Consult the editor-in-chief or the managing editor if in doubt.

GIFTS: UPI employees must maintain an arm's-length relationship with people or organizations in the news. Employees must not accept gifts from any sources whose activities fall or may be reasonably expected to fall within their own area of news coverage responsibility.

FREE TRAVEL: Accept no "junkets" except under unusual circumstances. This means that most are turned down. No trips in which travel or accommodations are provided by the host are to be accepted without prior approval of the president of UPI or the editor-in-chief.

COOPERATION: UPI policy forbids volunteering information or working for the CIA, FBI or any other governmental intelligence or law enforcement agency. Reporters and photographers are in frequent contact with the agencies' personnel and on occasion swap basic information, a common practice when several people who specialize in gathering facts witness an event. Covert or clandestine cooperation is another matter and we deplore the concept.

February 1981

THE SOCIETY OF PROFESSIONAL JOURNALISTS, SIGMA DELTA CHI CODE OF ETHICS

The Society of Professional Journalists, Sigma Delta Chi, believes the duty of journalists is to serve the truth.

We believe the agencies of mass communication are carriers of public discussion and information, acting on their Constitutional mandate and freedom to learn and report the facts.

We believe in public enlightenment as the forerunner of justice, and in our Constitutional role to seek the truth as part of the public's right to know the truth.

We believe those responsibilities carry obligations that require journalists to perform with intelligence, objectivity, accuracy and fairness.

To these ends, we declare acceptance of the standards of practice here set forth:

• **Responsibility:** The public's right to know of events of public importance and interest is the overriding mission of the mass media. The purpose of distributing news and enlightened opinion is to serve the general welfare. Journalists who use their professional status as representatives of the public for selfish or other unworthy motives violate a high trust.

• **Freedom of the Press:** Freedom of the press is to be guarded as an inalienable right of people in a free society. It carries with it the freedom and the responsibility to discuss, question and challenge actions and utterances of our government and of our public and private institutions. Journalists uphold the right to speak unpopular opinions and the privilege to agree with the majority.

• **Ethics:** Journalists must be free of obligation to any interest other than the public's right to know the truth.

 1. Gifts, favors, free travel, special treatment or privileges

can compromise the integrity of journalists and their employers. Nothing of value should be accepted.

2. Secondary employment, political involvement, holding public office and service in community organizations should be avoided if it compromises the integrity of journalists and their employers. Journalists and their employers should conduct their personal lives in a manner which protects them from conflict of interest, real or apparent. Their responsibilities to the public are paramount. That is the nature of their profession.

3. So-called news communications from private sources should not be published or broadcast without substantiation of their claims to news value.

4. Journalists will seek news that serves the public interest, despite the obstacles. They will make constant efforts to assure that the public's business is conducted in public and that public records are open to public inspection.

5. Journalists acknowledge the newsman's ethic of protecting confidential sources of information.

• **Accuracy and Objectivity:** Good faith with the public is the foundation of all worthy journalism.

1. Truth is our ultimate goal.

2. Objectivity in reporting the news is another goal, which serves as the mark of an experienced professional. It is a standard of performance toward which we strive. We honor those who achieve it.

3. There is no excuse for inaccuracies or lack of thoroughness.

4. Newspaper headlines should be fully warranted by the contents of the articles they accompany. Photographs and telecasts should give an accurate picture of an event and not highlight a minor incident out of context.

5. Sound practice makes clear distinction between news reports and expressions of opinion. News reports should be free of opinion or bias and represent all sides of an issue.

6. Partisanship in editorial comment which knowingly departs from the truth violates the spirit of American journalism.

7. Journalists recognize their responsibility for offering informed analysis, comment and editorial opinion on public events and issues. They accept the obligation to present such material by individuals whose competence, experience and judgment qualify them for it.

8. Special articles or presentations devoted to advocacy or the writer's own conclusions and interpretations should be labeled as such.

• **Fair Play:** Journalists at all times will show respect for the dignity, privacy, rights and well-being of people encountered in the course of gathering and presenting the news.

1. The news media should not communicate unofficial charges affecting reputation or moral character without giving the accused a chance to reply.

2. The news media must guard against invading a person's right to privacy.

3. The media should not pander to morbid curiosity about details of vice and crime.

4. It is the duty of news media to make prompt and complete correction of their errors.

5. Journalists should be accountable to the public for their reports and the public should be encouraged to voice its grievances against the media. Open dialogue with our readers, viewers and listeners should be fostered.

• **Pledge:** Journalists should actively censure and try to prevent violations of these standards, and they should encourage their observance by all newspeople. Adherence to this code of ethics is intended to preserve the bond of mutual trust and respect between American journalists and the American people.

Adopted by the 1973 national convention.

ASNE STATEMENT OF PRINCIPLES

PREAMBLE

The First Amendment, protecting freedom of expression from abridgment by any law, guarantees to the people through their press a constitutional right, and thereby places on newspaper people a particular responsibility.

Thus journalism demands of its practitioners not only industry and knowledge but also the pursuit of a standard of integrity proportionate to the journalist's singular obligation.

To this end the American Society of Newspaper Editors sets forth this Statement of Principles as a standard encouraging the highest ethical and professional performance.

ARTICLE I: RESPONSIBILITY

The primary purpose of gathering and distributing news and opinion is to serve the general welfare by informing the people and enabling them to make judgments on the issues of the time. Newspapermen and women who abuse the power of their professional role for selfish motives or unworthy purposes are faithless to that public trust.

The American press was made free not just to inform or just to serve as a forum for debate but also to bring an independent scrutiny to bear on the forces of power in the society, including the conduct of official power at all levels of government.

ARTICLE II: FREEDOM OF THE PRESS

Freedom of the press belongs to the people. It must be defended against encroachment or assault from any quarter, public or private.

Journalists must be constantly alert to see that the public's business is conducted in public. They must be vigilant against all who would exploit the press for selfish purposes.

ARTICLE III: INDEPENDENCE

Journalists must avoid impropriety and the appearance of impropriety as well as any conflict of interest or the appearance of conflict. They should neither accept anything nor pursue any activity that might compromise or seem to compromise their integrity.

ARTICLE IV: TRUTH AND ACCURACY

Good faith with the reader is the foundation of good journalism. Every effort must be made to assure that the news content is accurate, free from bias and in context, and that all sides are presented fairly. Editorials, analytical articles and commentary should be held to the same standards of accuracy with respect to facts as news reports.

Significant errors of fact, as well as errors of omission, should be corrected promptly and prominently.

ARTICLE V: IMPARTIALITY

To be impartial does not require the press to be unquestioning or to refrain from editorial expression. Sound practice, however, demands a clear distinction for the reader between news reports and opinion. Articles that contain opinion or personal interpretation should be clearly identified.

ARTICLE VI: FAIR PLAY

Journalists should respect the rights of people involved in the news, observe the common standards of decency and stand accountable to the public for the fairness and accuracy of their news reports.

Persons publicly accused should be given the earliest opportunity to respond.

Pledges of confidentiality to news sources must be honored at all costs, and therefore should not be given lightly. Unless there is clear and pressing need to maintain confidences, sources of information should be identified.

. . .

These principles are intended to preserve, protect and strengthen the bond of trust and respect between American journalists and the American people, a bond that is essential to sustain the grant of freedom entrusted to both by the nation's founders.

This Statement of Principles was adopted by the ASNE Board of Directors, Oct. 23, 1975; it supplants the 1922 Code of Ethics ("Canons of Journalism").

ASNE's Officers and Directors 1980-1981

OFFICERS

President: Thomas Winship, *The Boston Globe*
Vice President: Michael J. O'Neill, *New York Daily News*
Secretary: John C. Quinn, *Gannett Newspapers*
Treasurer: Creed C. Black, *Lexington (Ky.) Herald and Leader*

OTHER BOARD MEMBERS

Charles W. Bailey, *Minneapolis Tribune*
Judith W. Brown, *The Herald,* New Britain, Conn.
Anthony Day, *Los Angeles Times*
Michael Gartner, *The Des Moines Register and Tribune*
Tina Hills, *El Mundo,* San Juan, P.R.
William H. Hornby, *The Denver Post*
Larry Jinks, *Knight-Ridder Newspapers*
Clayton Kirkpatrick, *Chicago Tribune*
Edward D. Miller, *The Morning Call,* Allentown, Pa.
Charles S. Rowe, *The Free Lance-Star,* Fredericksburg, Va.
Claude Sitton, *The News and Observer/The Raleigh Times*
Richard D. Smyser, *The Oak Ridger,* Oak Ridge, Tenn.

The Ethics Committee

Chairman: Claude Sitton, *The News and Observer/The Raleigh Times*
Barry Bingham, Jr., *The Courier-Journal and The Louisville Times*
Robert Chandler, *The Bulletin,* Bend, Ore.
William C. Heine, *London (Ont.) Free Press*
William K. Hosokawa, *The Denver Post*
Frank McCulloch, *McClatchy Newspapers*
Joe Murray, *The Lufkin (Tex.) News*
Robert H. Phelps, *The Boston Globe*
James O. Powell, *Arkansas Gazette*
Walter Rugaber, *Greensboro (N.C.) Daily News and Record*
Charlotte Saikowski, *The Christian Science Monitor*
Donald J. Sterling, *Oregon Journal*
Robert Wills, *The Milwaukee Journal*

Index

Accident photographs, 60-63
Advocate role, 44-45
  defined, 45
Affirmative action
  as news policy, 47
Agnew, Spiro, 16
Alternative journalists, 47
Alienating sources, 8
Anonymous quotes, 47-48
Anonymous sources
  and confidentiality pledge, 64-65
  excessive reliance on, 47-48
Anti-Semitic leader case, 56
Appearance of impropriety, 25, 48
ASNE Washington meeting, 27
Associated Press, 63
Associated Press Managing Editors
  Assn., 60
  and picture survey, 60-61

Bar-press committees, 20-21
Basic ethic of journalism, 25
Bay of Pigs, 8
Bias in the news, 38-40
Boston schools, 39-40
Business editor
  abuse of role, 6
Byrne, Jane, 16

Canadian embassy, 9
Carter, Jimmy, 18
Cause of death
  in obituaries, 53
Central Intelligence Agency, 9
Change of venue, 21
Chicago police officer, 26
Chicago Sun-Times, 10
  and Mirage case, 10-11
Chicago Tribune, 16
Civic corruption
  Mirage case, 10-11
Civic organizations
  and conflict of interest, 28-32
Cleaning up quotations, 40
Closed judicial proceedings, 19-21
Closed meetings, 15-16
Cockfight story, 36
Commission on Freedom of the
  Press, 43
Communist Party, 55
Communist Workers Party, 58
Composite figure, 47
Composite photographs, 63
Concealing reporters' identity, 11

Confidentiality pledges
  qualified, 65
  risks involved, 65
  when to give, 64-65
Conflict of interest, 25-32
  ASNE members, 27
  civic organizations, 28-32
  editor, 27
  editorial writer, 27
  food editors, 27
  holding public office, 29-30
  political involvement, 29-30
  publisher, 12
  questions for journalists, 28, 32
  social contacts, 31-32
  sportswriters, 26-27
  travel writers, 27
  worthy causes, 30-32
  writing contests, 27
Contests for journalists, 27
Correction of errors, 37-38
  burying of, 37
  incidence, 38
  standing head, 37-38
  survey of editors, 38
Creating news, 22-23
Cropping photographs, 63
Crusades, 10-11

Dana, Charles, 52
Deception by reporters
  Mirage case, 10-11
  Three Mile Island, 11
  posing as doctor, 11
Deck-stacking in news, 39
Delay of trial, 21
Demonstrators
  and the press, 21-23
"Don't-rock-the-boat" policy, 7

Editorial writer
  abuse of role, 7
  as advocate, 45
  and conflict of interest, 27
Editorializing
  in news columns, 6, 38-40, 43-46
Entrapment
  Mirage case, 10-11
Errors
  correction of, 37-38
  effect on readers, 35-36
  survey, 38
Exploiting personal tragedy, 52-55, 60-63

INDEX

Exploiting the press, 21-22
  reporters as exploiters, 22-23
Fact errors, *see* Errors
Faked news stories, 36
Favors and gifts, 25-28
Fiction writer's devices, 46-47
First Amendment
  and access to trials, 19-20
  and confidentiality pledge, 65
  and pre-trial publicity, 20-21
Florida gambling, 31
Food writers, 22, 27
  conflict of interest, 27
Ford, Gerald, 58
Fourth Estate, 5
Freebies, 25-28
  questions for journalists, 28
Freedom of the press
  and defense of, 15-17

Gannett, Inc. v. DePasquale, 19-21
Gatekeeper role, 44-45
Gay persons in news, *see* Homosexuals
"Get It First, But First Get It Right," 36
Gifts and favors, 25-28
Girl in burning fraternity house, 52

Handouts, 13
Holding public office
  arguments for, 30
  as conflict of interest, 29-30
Homosexuals
  when to use identification, 58-59
  political candidate, 59
  veteran who saved President, 58-59
Honorific titles in news, 57
Hostages at U.S. embassy, 9
  and press coverage, 21-22
  escape of, 9
Hyping quotations, 7

Identifying figures in the news, 57
  homosexuals, 58-59
  racial minorities, 57-58
Influencing news
  by ownership, 11-13
International News Service, 36
Interpretive reporting, 43-46
Invasion of privacy, *see* Privacy
Investigative journalism, 11-12, 55-57
Iran
  hostage rescue attempt, 62-63
  militants, 9
Israel, 27
"It all begins with a cigar," 26

Jackson, Henry, 39
Janowitz, Morris, 44-45
Journalism Quarterly, 45

Kennedy, John F., 8
Ku Klux Klan, 58

Labor leader as Communist case, 55-56
Letters to editor
  faked, 7
Lewiston Tribune, The (Idaho), 32
Litmus questions, 28, 32
Los Angeles Times, 31

McCarthy, Joseph R., 10
Media events, 21-22
Middle East, 27
Mirage, The, 10-11
Misleading photographs, 39-40, 63
Mount St. Helens, 62

National chicken cooking contest, 27
National Review, 46
National security
  and Pentagon Papers, 10
  and the news, 8-10
  in *The Progressive* case, 9
New Journalism, 43-47
New Republic, The, 46
News
  exploitation of, 6
  suppressing of, 8-9
  in wartime, 8
Newsgathering methods
  concealing reporter's identity, 11
  and Mirage case, 10-11
  and Pentagon Papers, 10
Newspaper owners
  on corporate boards, 12
  influencing news, 12
News photographs, *see* Photographs
Newsroom searches, 18
  1980 law, 18
News sources
  cultivation, 8
  relationship with reporters, 8
Newsworthiness
  and right of privacy, 51-63
New York Times, The, 8-9, 30, 43
North Carolina, 58

Obituaries
  and cause of death, 53
Objectivity, 43-48
  as ideal, 44
Open-meeting law, 15
Opinion in news, 46
Ownership interlocks, 11-13
Ownership of press
  by oil company, 12

Padding a story, 48
Partisan press, 46
Patterson, Eugene, 31
Pentagon Papers, 10
Photographs, 39-40, 60-63
  closeup, 60
  composites, 63
  cropping, 63
  faked, 63
  fire escape fall, 61-62
  grieving father, 60-61

high-wire artist's fall, 62
Iran hostage rescue attempt, 62-63
misleadingly captioned, 39
school desegregation, 39-40
senator's "crowd," 39
unpublished negatives, subpoenaed, 17-19
volcano victim, 62
water skier, 61
Planted questions, 23
Political involvement
 as conflict of interest, 29-30
Politicians
 and the press, 21
 relatives of, in the news, 54-55
Post-Watergate era, 55
Power forces in society, 11
Power of press abused, 6
Press
 as catalyst, 67
 role of, 5, 6, 67
Press-public interdependence, 67
Pre-trial hearings, 19-20
 and news coverage, 20-21
Prior restraint, 9
Privacy, invasion of
 by photographs, 60-63
 children of celebrities, 54-55
 dying girl, 53-54
 food stamps, 54-55
 girl in burning fraternity house, 52
 murdered prostitute, 52-53
 prison record, 56-57
 racist leader, 56
 senator's son, daughter, 54-55
 union official, 55-56
Privacy, right of
 and newsworthiness, 51-63
Professional role, abuse of
 by business writer, 6
 by editorial writer, 7
 by newspaper chain owner, 6
 by publisher, 6
 by reporters, 6, 7
 by sportswriter, 7
Progressive, The
 and hydrogen bomb story, 9
Prostitute murder case, 52-53
Public officeholding by journalists, 29-30
Public opinion
 and press freedom, 16-17
 of press, 16-17
Public relations releases, 13
Pulitzer Prize, 62

Quotations
 boiled-down, 64
 correcting grammar, 40, 64
 distortion of, 64
 editing, 64
 how to use, 63-64
 hyping, 7
 made-up, 64
Racial identification in news, 57-58

Railroading press releases, 13
Reader complaints, 53, 62
Reconstructed conversations, 46
Reporters
 abusing roles, 6, 7
 adopting other roles, 11
 concealing identity, 11
 co-opted by sources, 8
 models, 44-45
 notes, subpoenaed, 17-19
Responsibility of press, abuse of
 by newspaper chain owner, 6
 by omission, 7
 by publisher, 6
Reston, James, 43
Richmond Newspapers, Inc. v. Virginia, 19-21
Role of the press, 5, 6
Rosenthal, A.M., 30
Rotary meeting, 26
Royster, Vermont, 5, 67

St. Petersburg Times, 31
San Francisco, 58, 59
"Sanitized" journalist, 31
School busing photographs, 39-40
Scrutiny of government, avoided, 7
Sequestering of the jury, 21
Sexist references in news, 57
Shield laws, 65
Sixth Amendment, 19-21
Sportswriters as scorers, 26-27
Stanford Daily, The, 18
Star-spangled pickle, 36
Subpoenas of press material
 incidence, 17
 resistance to, 18-19
Suicide threat case, 56
Supreme Court
 and confidentiality pledge, 65
 and pre-trial hearings, 19-21
Suppressing news
 hostage escape, 9
 hydrogen bomb story, 9
 in wartime, 8

Three Mile Island, 11
Travel writers and junkets, 27
Trials, Supreme Court decisions, 19-21

United Way, 32
University of Chicago, 44

Vietnam
 and Pentagon Papers, 10

Wall Street Journal, The, 5, 38, 67
War correspondent, 26
Washington, D.C., 52
Washington state, 62
Watchdog function, 7, 8, 13, 16-17
Watergate, 16, 65
Weighing values, 51
 anti-Semitic leader case, 56
 photographs, 60-63
 prison record case, 56-57
 union leader case, 55-56
White House, 59
Winter Olympics, 28